Civic Du

Working Together

T0024883

Shirin Shamsi

Reader Consultants

Cheryl Norman Lane, M.A.Ed.
Classroom Teacher
Chino Valley Unified School District

Jennifer M. Lopez, M.S.Ed., NBCT
Teacher Specialist—History/Social Studies
Norfolk Public Schools

iCivics Consultants

Emma Humphries, Ph.D.
Chief Education Officer

Taylor Davis, M.T.
Director of Curriculum and Content

Natacha Scott, MAT
Director of Educator Engagement

Publishing Credits

Rachelle Cracchiolo, M.S.Ed., *Publisher*
Emily R. Smith, M.A.Ed., *VP of Content Development*
Véronique Bos, *Creative Director*
Dona Herweck Rice, *Senior Content Manager*
Dani Neiley, *Associate Content Specialist*
Fabiola Sepulveda, *Series Designer*

Image Credits: pp.6–9 Ana Sebastian; p.12 Library of Congress [LC-USZ6-656];
p.13 (top) Library of Congress [LC-DIG-ppmsca-23661]; p.14 U.S. National
Archives; p.15 Bettman/Getty Images; p.17 Peter Newark American Pictures/
Bridgeman Images; p.20 David Hume Kennerly/Getty Images; p.21 Getty Images/
Mark Wilson; p.23 (top) Fabiola Sepulveda; p.24 Zuma Press/Alamy; p.25 (top)
Farooq Naeem/AFP/Gettyimages; all other images from iStock and/or Shuterstock

Library of Congress Cataloging-in-Publication Data

Names: Shamsi, Shirin, author.
Title: Civic duty : working together / Shirin Shamsi.
Description: Huntington Beach, CA : Teacher Created Materials, 2021. |
  Includes index. | Audience: Grades 2-3 | Summary: "Everyone has a civic
  duty. It is a responsibility of all citizens. When they serve their
  communities, they can improve things. When everyone works together, we
  can all learn from each other. When people fulfill their civic duties,
  everyone benefits"-- Provided by publisher.
Identifiers: LCCN 2020016196 (print) | LCCN 2020016197 (ebook) | ISBN
  9781087605135 (paperback) | ISBN 9781087619378 (ebook)
Subjects: LCSH: Civics--Juvenile literature. | Responsibility--Juvenile literature.
Classification: LCC JK1759 .S53 2021 (print) | LCC JK1759 (ebook) | DDC 323.6/50973--dc23
LC record available at https://lccn.loc.gov/2020016196
LC ebook record available at https://lccn.loc.gov/2020016197

TCM | Teacher Created Materials

5482 Argosy Avenue
Huntington Beach, CA 92649-1039
www.tcmpub.com

ISBN 978-1-0876-0513-5
© 2022 Teacher Created Materials, Inc.

Table of Contents

What Is Civic Duty?

Have you ever seen a tapestry? It is made of many colors and textures. The threads are joined together, stitch by stitch. When those threads are woven, they become one work of art.

Civic duty is like that. This is the responsibility each person has for the whole community. Just like a tapestry, people come together to serve their communities. They can serve on juries, helping to make courtroom decisions. They pay taxes. They can vote. They can serve in the **armed forces**. They can follow laws and know their rights. All these things are part of civic duties.

You may not be able to do all these things yet. But there are other ways you can serve your community. You have your own civic duties.

These woven threads form a tapestry.

These people serve on a jury.

Where Did It Come From?

The word *civics* comes from two Latin words or phrases. The first is *civis*, a citizen of ancient Rome. The second is *corona civica*, a word for a type of crown. The crown was given to a person who saved someone's life. It showed that they helped people in their community.

Ali's Morning

"Yes! If I run, I won't be late to school again," Ali yelled. He grabbed his backpack and bolted out the door and down the street, running as fast as his legs could carry him. He had already been given a warning for being late. He might get kicked off the track team! This was his last chance, and he wasn't going to blow it.

The cool breeze whipped Ali's hair as he picked up speed and imagined he was a champion runner on a racetrack. Track was his favorite sport. Ali sighed. *One day*, he promised himself, *I'll be an Olympic champion runner.* But first, he needed to get to school on time.

Ali stopped suddenly when he saw Mr. Patel, his elderly neighbor, lying in the middle of the road. A car was coming. The driver might not see him on the road!

Ali grabbed his yellow backpack and waved it above his head as he stepped into the road. He stood by Mr. Patel and kept waving hard until the oncoming car stopped. Then, Ali gently helped his neighbor stand. Ali picked up the walking stick that lay on the ground and handed it back to Mr. Patel. Ali walked Mr. Patel to the sidewalk, making sure he wasn't hurt.

"Thank you, son," said Mr. Patel. "Go on now, or you'll be late for school."

Ali sighed softly. He already knew he was late. And he knew he might get kicked off the track team. As sad as Ali was, he also knew he had done the right thing. He swung his backpack over his shoulder and ran the rest of the way to school.

Back to Nonfiction

You and Your Civic Duty

You belong to many places. You belong to a family and a group of friends. You belong to a school and a community. You also belong to larger places, such as your state, your country, and even the planet. You have a duty to help and serve all those places.

There are many ways you can help. Like a caring family member does, a good community member looks out for others. You may help an elderly neighbor shovel snow. Or you may tutor younger students. Everyone can do something. Small things add up to make a big difference. When people come together, great things can happen!

Everyone can and should fulfill their civic duties. Some people go above and beyond to improve the world around them. They show what it means to do their civic duty for the good of all. The next chapters highlight some of these civic leaders.

Which Do I Use?

Some people use the term "civic responsibility." Others call it "civic virtues." You may also see "civic engagement." All these terms mean mostly the same thing. They mean that people have responsibilities.

☆Think and Talk

In what ways are these
children showing their civic
responsibility? Can you spot
more than one way?

Famous Figures

> "Alone we can do so little;
> together we can do so much."
> —Helen Keller

Helen Keller became very sick when she was a baby. The illness took away her hearing and her eyesight. Her world was dark and silent. As she grew up, she worked to improve her remaining **senses** of touch, smell, and taste. She learned to communicate with others. Even with all the problems she faced, Keller rose to the challenge.

Keller uses her hand to know what her friend is saying.

Keller worked to make other people's lives better. She wrote books about peace. She traveled the world and inspired people to fight for the rights of women and children. People listened when she spoke. She changed the way people thought about **disabilities**. With courage, she improved the world around her.

Keller's Abilities

Keller learned to read **braille**. She touched people's faces to read their lips. She learned to speak by moving her mouth as she felt other people do. She learned to feel the vibrations of movement to know when someone was near.

> **"A life is not important except in the impact it has on other lives."**
> —**Jackie Robinson**

Jackie Robinson was a great baseball player. He was **recruited** to play in Major League Baseball (MLB). It had long been against the rules for African American players to do this. Robinson used this opportunity to break down barriers.

It was not easy for him. People attacked him. They yelled at him and insulted him. Though it was hard, Robinson held in his anger. He did not fight back. He tried to ignore them and focus on baseball. It took all his strength to keep calm. Robinson knew he was playing for more than just himself. He thought of others before his own wants.

His determination and patience paid off. He won awards and was one of baseball's greatest hitters. Even more importantly, he became a **civil rights** hero.

Retiring Robinson

In 1997, the MLB said that Robinson's number would be **retired**. That meant that no new players could wear the number 42. It was a way of honoring Robinson. He is the only MLB player to have his number retired for all teams.

Robinson gives a civil rights speech in 1960.

Think and Talk

How do you think the author feels about civic duty? What evidence in the text supports your idea?

TIME TO SCORE FOR CIVIL RIGHTS

GIVE-JOIN NAACP

Powerful Politicians

> "It is the first responsibility of every citizen to question authority."
>
> —Benjamin Franklin

Benjamin Franklin is one of the **Founders** of our country. He is also known as the Founder of Civics. Franklin spent most of his life in civic service. He hoped to make life better for all people.

Franklin valued hard work. He convinced people to work together to serve their communities. He raised money for better roads. He helped start a college. Franklin even created one of the country's first fire services.

Franklin also valued education. When he learned that people could not afford to buy books, he wondered how they would learn. So, he opened the first lending library. His life of service improved the lives of many people. His ideas continue to improve lives today.

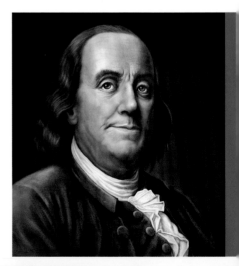

Franklin in 1736

Franklin's Fire Club

Franklin's fire service was called the Union Fire Company. Members of the club promised to help one another put out fires. The club was a great success. Soon, fire clubs opened all over Franklin's city.

> **"I believe in the promise of America."**
> **—Ileana Ros-Lehtinen**

Ileana Ros-Lehtinen was born in Cuba. She moved to the United States when she was seven. She worked hard and was a good student. In time, she earned an advanced degree in education. Then, she opened her own school. But she was not done. She wanted to have a bigger civic impact.

Ros-Lehtinen ran for a seat in the Florida Senate. She won! Seven years later, she won a special election. She became the first Latina elected to the U.S. **Congress**. She was also the first person from Cuba elected to Congress. And she was the first Republican woman from her state to serve in this way.

In all, Ros-Lehtinen was elected to Congress 14 times. She retired in 2019.

Ros-Lehtinen worked hard for the people of her state.

> **"We don't accomplish anything in this world alone."**
> **—Sandra Day O'Connor**

Sandra Day O'Connor loved horses and the land. As a child, she helped on her family's **ranch**. She saw that small choices they made on the ranch could have a big impact. O'Connor noticed that the same was true for public lands near the ranch. Small government steps to care for the land had a big impact too. She thought that was a good thing.

O'Connor in front of the Supreme Court building in 1981.

O'Connor went to college and studied law. But after graduating, no one would hire a woman lawyer. So, O'Connor practiced law for free. Later, she worked as a lawyer for the Arizona state government. Then, she was elected to the Arizona state senate. Through hard work, she became one of its highest-ranking members. Then, in 1981, she was **nominated** to the U.S. Supreme Court. That is the highest court in the country. O'Connor was the first woman to serve on the U.S. Supreme Court. She served on the court for 25 years. After retiring, O'Connor started an organization that makes video games to teach kids about civics!

O'Connor in 2005

Students Who Serve

> "I've learned you are never too small
> to make a difference."
> —Greta Thunberg

Greta Thunberg was eight years old when she saw a film at school. The film showed how **climate change** affects all living things. The suffering of polar bears moved her to tears. She could not stop thinking about it. It made her sad. It also made her mad. She wanted to know how people could help. Over the next few years, she read books and learned more about climate change. She could not accept that nothing was being done about such an important problem.

Thunberg's actions inspired millions of people to protest climate change.

GRETA
THUNBERG

THE POWER
OF YOUTH

Thunberg's Passion

When Thunberg was young, she was told she had Asperger's syndrome. People with Asperger's tend to focus on one idea at a time. For Thunberg, she focused on climate change.

Thunberg was *TIME* magazine's Person of the Year in 2019.

Thunberg decided to take matters into her own hands. She sat outside government offices in Sweden with a poster board that read "School Strike for Climate." People listened. They wanted to help too, and a global movement began. Leaders of nations around the world were inspired to pay attention because of one young person.

> "Together we can cultivate peace, nurture hope, and change the world—one child at a time."
> —Pennies for Peace

In 1995, two teachers heard a speech about life for many children in Pakistan. They wanted to help. The teachers shared what they had learned with their students. The students learned that not all children could go to school. Some places did not have school buildings or basic school supplies, such as pencils.

students in Pakistan

The students decided to help. They collected lots of change. Their collections helped pay to build a school! But the students did not stop there. They spread the word about their project. Across the country, other students collected change. They sent the money to people in other countries who were in need. The students formed a group called Pennies for Peace. Today, hundreds of schools are part of Pennies for Peace.

Even More

Pennies for Peace does even more than build schools and buy supplies. They support teachers and provide **scholarships** for students. They offer job training for women. They offer public healthcare too!

Doing Your Part

A good community member cares about the world around them. They perform their civic duties to make the world better. We all have the power to make a difference. We just have to take it one step at a time.

As you get older, you will have more and more civic duties. You will have to pay more taxes as an adult. You may serve in the armed forces. But, even now, there are responsibilities that you have to your community and your country. You should stay informed about what is happening around the world. You can speak out against injustice. You can stand up for what you believe is right. All these things matter. All these things can make a difference in the world.

These people recycle things.

Imagine yourself by a pond. Now, imagine throwing a pebble into the pond. What do you see? First, there's a splash as the pebble cuts through the water. Then, there are ripples. At first, the ripples are small circles. Then, they grow wider and wider as the impact of one small pebble has an effect on the whole pond.

Think and Talk

How do you think the author feels about civic duty? What evidence in the text supports your idea?

Like the pebble's ripple effect, small things matter. Small actions have big impacts. All people can affect their neighborhoods and wider communities. Together, people can support one another. Together, people can show they care. Together, people can make the world better.

Glossary

armed forces—the military organizations of a country, such as the army, navy, and air force

braille—a system of writing in which letters are represented by raised dots

civil rights—the rights that all people should have regardless of things such as religion, race, or gender

climate change—the change in the world's temperature that is believed to be caused by the increase of certain gases in the atmosphere

Congress—made up of the Senate and the House of Representatives, it is the branch of the government that makes laws

disabilities—conditions that limit or damage people's mental or physical abilities

Founders—the people who played an important role in creating the U.S. government

nominated—formally chosen for a position, job, or office

ranch—a large farm where animals are raised

recruited—found and persuaded

retired—taken out of use, production, or service

scholarships—money given to students to help pay for their education

senses—the five natural powers (smell, sight, hearing, touch, and taste) through which people receive information about the world around them

Index

Civics in Action

Everyone has a civic duty. People fulfill their civic duties by following community rules and voting. They follow laws and volunteer in their communities. Some people even help the world!

1. Think about something you would like to see happen at your school. It may be a change, a special event, or a special project.

2. Brainstorm how to get your idea done.

3. Make a design plan for how to get your idea accomplished.

4. Share your idea with a friend to see if they like it or have any suggestions to make it better.

5. If you feel inspired, put your plan into action!